History Makers

Air Pioneers

Neil Morris

Chrysalis Education

US Publication copyright © 2003 Chrysalis Education
International copyright reserved in all countries.
No part of this book may be reproduced in any form without written permission from the publisher.

Distributed in the United States by
Smart Apple Media
1980 Lookout Drive
North Mankato, MN 56003

ISBN 1-93233-381-9

Library of Congress Control Number 2003 102634

Editorial Manager: Joyce Bentley
Assistant Editor: Clare Chambers
Editor: Rosalind Beckman
Designer: Sarah Crouch
Picture Researcher: Jenny Barlow

Printed in Hong Kong
10 9 8 7 6 5 4 3 2 1

Picture credits:
B = bottom; L = left; R = right; T = top.
Cover front and back Philip Jarrett 4 Corbis/Bettmann 5 T Mary Evans B Hulton Archive 6 Hulton Archive 7 T Mary Evans B Science Museum/SSPL 8 Science Museum/SSPL 8-9 Philip Jarrett 9 and 10 Mary Evans 11 T Rex/Timepix/Mansell B Chrysalis Images 12 T Mary Evans B Philip Jarrett 13 Philip Jarrett 14 Hulton Archive 15 T Mary Evans B Philip Jarrett 16 Mary Evans 17 T Philip Jarrett B Mary Evans 18 Mary Evans 19 T Science Museum/SSPL B Hulton Archive 20-21 Philip Jarrett 21 T Philip Jarrett B TRH Pictures 22 Hulton Archive 23 T Corbis/Minnesota Historical Society B Mary Evans 24 Mary Evans 25 L Corbis/Bettmann R Mary Evans 26 Hulton Archive 27 T Hulton Archive B Corbis/Bettmann 28 T Hulton Archive B Mary Evans 30 Hulton Archive 31 T Science Museum/SSPL B Corbis/Bettmann 32 Hulton Archive 33 T Mary Evans B Hulton Archive 34 Rex/Timepix/Scherschel 35 T The Art Archive/Manoir du Clos Lucé/Dagli Orti B Philip Jarrett 36 Philip Jarrett 37 T Corbis/Steve Starr B TRH Pictures 38 Hulton Archive 39 T Corbis/Bettmann B Hulton Archive 40 T Science Museum/SSPL B Hulton Archive 41 TRH Pictures 42 Rex 43 T SPL/NASA B Hulton Archive 44 Rex /Timepix/Air Force 45 T Reuters/Sam Mircovich B Hulton Archive.
All reasonable efforts have been made to trace the relevant copyright holders of the images contained within this book. If we were unable to reach you, please contact Chrysalis Education.

Contents

Introduction	4
George Cayley	6
The Wright brothers	10
Louis Blériot	14
Alcock and Brown	18
Charles Lindbergh	22
Amelia Earhart	26
Amy Johnson	30
Igor Sikorsky	34
Frank Whittle	38
Chuck Yeager	42
Glossary	46
Index	48

INTRODUCTION

Today, it is easy to forget that the first powered planes took off only 100 years ago. Since then, the amazing developments in human flight have depended on the skill and courage of many people. In this book, we look at the fascinating lives of ten of the world's greatest air pioneers.

Ancient ideas

People have dreamed of flying for thousands of years. The Greeks told stories of brave men who made wings and tried to fly like birds. Kites were invented in ancient China and they helped scientists to learn about how things fly. By the sixteenth century, the great Italian artist and scientist Leonardo da Vinci was drawing flying machines with flapping wings. Inventors had lots of ideas, but practical people were needed to make them work.

First flyers

The first machines to take people up into the air were hot-air balloons. Following the first flights in France, people developed strange-shaped **airships**. But the problem with these machines was that they were dependent on the wind and difficult to control. Other pioneers began working on the idea of aircraft with wings. One of the greatest of these early inventors was Sir George Cayley, who built the first successful man-carrying **glider**.

Powered flight

Cayley realised that to fly any great distance aircraft needed a power source, or engine. At the beginning of the twentieth century, powered aeroplanes with **propellers** at last took to the sky.

This newspaper reported the Wrights' historic first flight as being much longer than it really was. It was such big news!

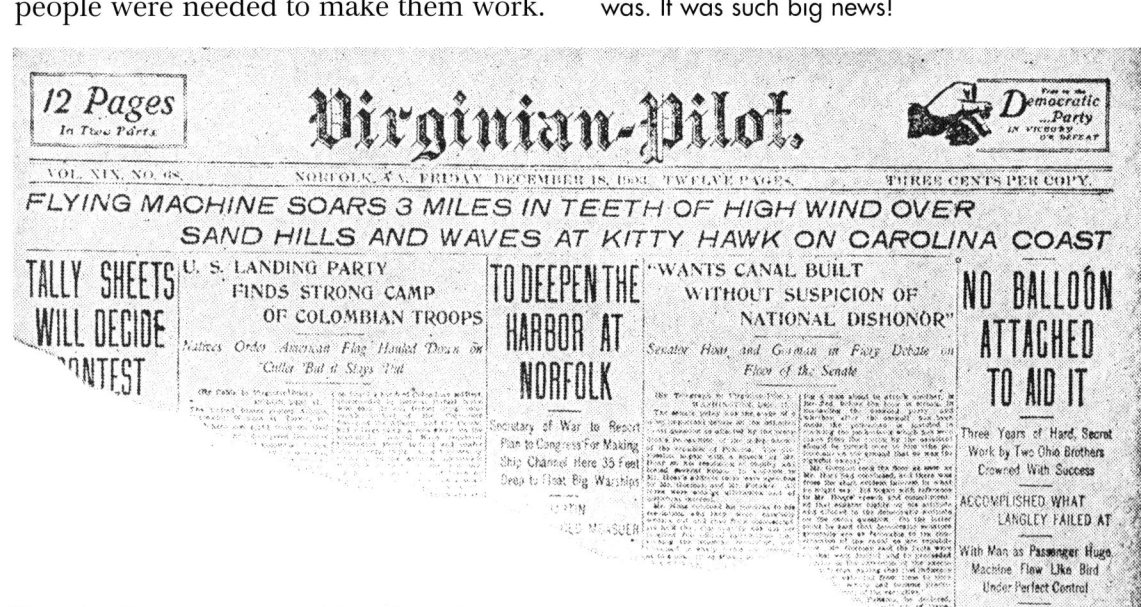

INTRODUCTION

This Italian advertising poster dates from 1928. It shows how popular the idea of flight became during the 1920s.

Soaring success
The first pioneers to fly a powered plane in controlled flight were two American bicycle-makers, the Wright brothers. Their historic achievement in 1903 encouraged other inventors and engineers to become **aviators**.

Giant airships filled with hydrogen gas were developed during the 1930s. This is the German *Hindenburg* flying over New York.

Breaking records
Many great aviators spent their time trying to fly faster, higher, and farther – and pioneers such as Blériot, Alcock, Brown, and Lindbergh were soon breaking records. At the same time, they captured the public imagination and made **aviation** popular when most ordinary people could still only dream of flying. Two great female aviators, Amelia Earhart and Amy Johnson, showed that women could push flying boundaries, too. Like many daring airmen, they lost their lives in the process.

Technical advances
Other pioneers concentrated on advancing different ways of flying. Igor Sikorsky designed a variety of planes, but he is best known for developing the helicopter. By the 1940s, Sir Frank Whittle had invented the jet engine, which changed flying forever. This left one barrier still to break – the sound barrier. It took a rocket-powered plane and an extraordinary pilot, Charles Yeager, to achieve this in 1947.

George Cayley

1773–1857

British engineer and inventor Sir George Cayley was an early designer of flying machines. One of his greatest achievements was to build the first successful man-carrying glider.

George Cayley was the only son of Sir Thomas Cayley and his wife Isabella. The Cayley family lived at Brompton Hall, near Scarborough on the North Yorkshire coast of England. The young George, who had four sisters, was first sent to school in York and then educated by a private tutor. When he was 18, George went to Southgate, near London, to study chemistry and electricity under the careful eye of a church minister named George Cadogan Morgan.

Toys and models

When his father died in 1792, George succeeded him as **baronet** and became Sir George Cayley. Three years later, he married Sarah, the daughter of his first tutor. By then he was already working on various kinds of flying machines. He experimented with a Chinese "flying top", a toy helicopter that he had seen demonstrated. By 1799, he had designed a glider with fixed wings and special controls that helped it to fly.

Sir George Cayley was one of the greatest early pioneers, even through he never took to the air himself.

GEORGE CAYLEY

The Montgolfier brothers

In 1782, when George Cayley was just nine, two French brothers, Joseph-Michel Montgolfier (1740–1810) and Jacques-Etienne Montgolfier (1745–99), discovered that a paper bag filled with hot air rose into the sky. A year later they sent a sheep, a duck, and a rooster up in a hot air balloon. This encouraged the brothers to send up two men: a chemist named Pilâtre de Rozier and an army officer, the Marquis d'Arlandes. The two balloonists rose 300 ft into the air over Paris and stayed up for 25 minutes. On that day in 1783 they became the first people to fly above the earth.

Full-size glider

Cayley returned to his family home at Brompton Hall and used the large grounds to test out his ideas. He made models and kites, before building a full-size glider in 1809. Trials showed that this aircraft was strong and stable. No one flew in the glider, but Cayley claimed that when someone ran with it into a gentle breeze, it would lift into the air and carry the runner for a short distance. The inventor then explained the basic principles of airplane flight in a journal published in 1810. This article was reprinted in France and America well after its author's death.

The English-born engineer Lawrence Hargrave (1850–1915) understood the principles of flight as explained by Cayley. The structure of his box kite was used in some early planes.

Gunpowder and hot air

Although he continued to work with gliders, Cayley became convinced that a machine was needed to push airplanes along. He knew that a steam engine would be too heavy, so he experimented with other sources of energy. First, he tried an engine fueled by gunpowder and then he developed a hot-air engine. In 1820, he flew a model airship at Brompton, and he did further work comparing hot air and **hydrogen** as lifting gases.

First "flyer"

In 1849, Cayley built a full-size triplane glider, or "flyer" as he called it – and then flew it a few yards with a ten-year-old boy on board. Four years later, a new version became the first successful man-carrying glider in the world.

A modern replica of Cayley's "new flyer" of 1853 takes to the air.

A model of George Cayley's proposed "aerial carriage" of 1843. Cayley continued to modify it and six years later he built a full-size version.

The coachman's flight

Cayley took his "new flyer" to the top of a small valley near Brompton Hall. This was probably another **triplane** glider, with three small wheels for an **undercarriage**. Cayley persuaded his coachman to climb aboard. It was claimed that this historic flight covered a distance of up to nearly 1,500 ft, although experts think it may have been much shorter. Whatever its length, the flight certainly ended with a heavy landing. As he struggled out of the glider, the coachman cried: "Please, Sir George, I wish to give notice. I was hired to drive and not to fly!"

MP and university founder

Cayley served as an British **Member of Parliament** for Scarborough from 1832 to 1834. He wanted to help young people learn about science and engineering, and in 1838 he founded the Polytechnic Institution in London. The Polytechnic ran evening classes in general science, as well as courses in **navigation** and even railroad-engine driving. Over 150 years later, this important institution became the University of Westminster.

Other achievements

As well as his pioneering work in aviation, Sir George Cayley did research work and invented in many other areas. He supported engineers building a new drainage system to stop flooding in Yorkshire, developed the crawler tractor, worked on safety equipment for railroads and even made an artificial hand for one of his tenants. Cayley had ten children with his wife Sarah. When he died at the age of 83, he was succeeded as baronet by his son Digby.

Otto Lilienthal

Towards the end of the nineteenth century, the German engineer Otto Lilienthal (1848–1896) made more than 2,000 flights in his own gliders. Lilienthal built five **monoplane** gliders and two **biplane** gliders, which he steered by shifting his weight backward and forward. He survived several accidents and once managed to glide for more than 800 ft. He was killed when one of his aircraft crashed into a hillside.

The Wright Brothers

Wilbur Wright 1867–1912
Orville Wright 1871–1948

Wilbur and Orville Wright invented, built, and flew the world's first power-driven airplane. They made their historic flight in North Carolina in 1903.

Wilbur was born in Millville, Indiana, the third son of Milton Wright, a church minister, and his wife Susan. By the time Orville was born, the family had moved to Dayton, Ohio, where the minister edited a church newspaper. A sister, Katharine, was born in 1874. Their father was a well-read man, with a great interest in mechanics. Milton's enthusiasm was shared by their mother, who let her children use her kitchen for science experiments.

Printers and bicycle makers

The Wright brothers were great inventors: Orville had the ideas and Wilbur put them into practice. When given the job of folding copies of their father's newspaper, the brothers built a machine that enabled them to do this much faster. Then Orville persuaded Wilbur to help him build a printing press. When this worked well, the brothers opened a print shop. In 1892, they switched to repairing and selling bicycles. It was not long before they were making improvements to the bikes and then building their own.

Wilbur Wright (top) and his brother Orville worked brilliantly together as an inventing team.

Samuel Langley

Backed by the US government, American **physicist** Samuel Langley (1834–1906) built powered model airplanes in the 1890s, which he launched from his houseboat on the Potomac River. On December 8, 1903, nine days before the Wright brothers' success at Kitty Hawk, Langley tried to launch a full-size plane named *Aerodrome*. But it failed to take off and simply dropped into the river. Langley lost his government support and abandoned the project.

First flying experiments

The brothers read about Otto Lilienthal's gliding experiments and, after his death in 1896, they started their own flying experiments – first building a kite and then a full-scale glider. They found that the best place to fly was near the village of Kitty Hawk on the coast of North Carolina, where there were good winds and wide stretches of sand for soft landings. In 1900, they flew their glider there and very soon Wilbur was piloting it for flights of up to 400 ft.

The Wrights' Flyer

The brothers wanted to add an engine that was both powerful and light. They used bicycle chains to attach a gasoline engine to two wooden propellers behind the wings. Their plane, which they called *Flyer*, was a biplane. The pilot lay on the lower wing in a cradle. As he moved from side to side, the cradle pulled wires that twisted the wings slightly. This "wing-warping" system gave the pilot some steering control. After being held up by bad weather, the brothers were at last ready to fly.

First powered flight

On the morning of December 17, 1903 Orville piloted the plane for its first flight. He was **airborne** for 12 seconds and flew 120 ft. Then it was Wilbur's turn and he flew a little further. Orville increased the distance again on the third flight, and the fourth and final attempt was the most successful of all. Five locals watched as Wilbur flew for 59 seconds and covered 865 ft.

Wilbur watches as Orville takes off on the first powered flight at Kitty Hawk on that famous day in 1903.

AIR PIONEERS

The brilliant Brazilian aviator Alberto Santos-Dumont (1873–1932) built this tail-first, box-kite plane. In 1906, he won a prize in Paris for flying it 735 ft.

Improved designs

Over the next few years, the Wright brothers improved the design of their aircraft. By 1905, *Flyer III* could stay in the air for more than 38 minutes, turning and circling with ease. The brothers then took two years off from flying while they took out **patents** on their aircraft. This meant that others could not copy their work and they could make plans to sell their planes. By 1908, they were back with a modified *Flyer* that had upright seating for two. Wilbur shipped a plane to France and flew it there to promote sales, while Orville took part in U.S. Army trials.

A crashing success

During one of Orville's trial flights in Virginia, a propeller broke, causing the engine to cut out and the plane to dive to the ground. The crash killed the passenger, Lieutenant Thomas Selfridge, and Orville broke a leg and several ribs. All his other flights were successful, however, and the U.S. Army bought its first plane from the Wrights for $30,000. The brothers formed the Wright Company in 1909 to manufacture airplanes and give flying exhibitions.

The Wrights' Model A first flew in 1908.

Flying and training

In 1909, Wilbur flew a Wright plane over New York, and this gave many thousands of people their first ever glimpse of powered flight. The brothers were also presented with medals by President William Howard Taft at the White House. They opened an aircraft factory in Dayton, Ohio, as well as a flying school. There they trained Henry H. Arnold, who later went on to command the U.S. Army Air Forces. All these activities made more and more people interested in airplanes.

Orville carries on

After Wilbur died of typhoid fever in 1912, aged just 45, Orville carried on their business. During World War I, he worked as a consulting engineer and in 1920 President Woodrow Wilson appointed him to the U.S. National Advisory Committee for **Aeronautics**. Orville always preferred inventing and flying to making speeches. When once asked to speak to a large group of people in France, he said: "The bird that does the most talking – the parrot – cannot fly very high." Thirty-six years after his brother's death, Orville Wright died of a heart attack.

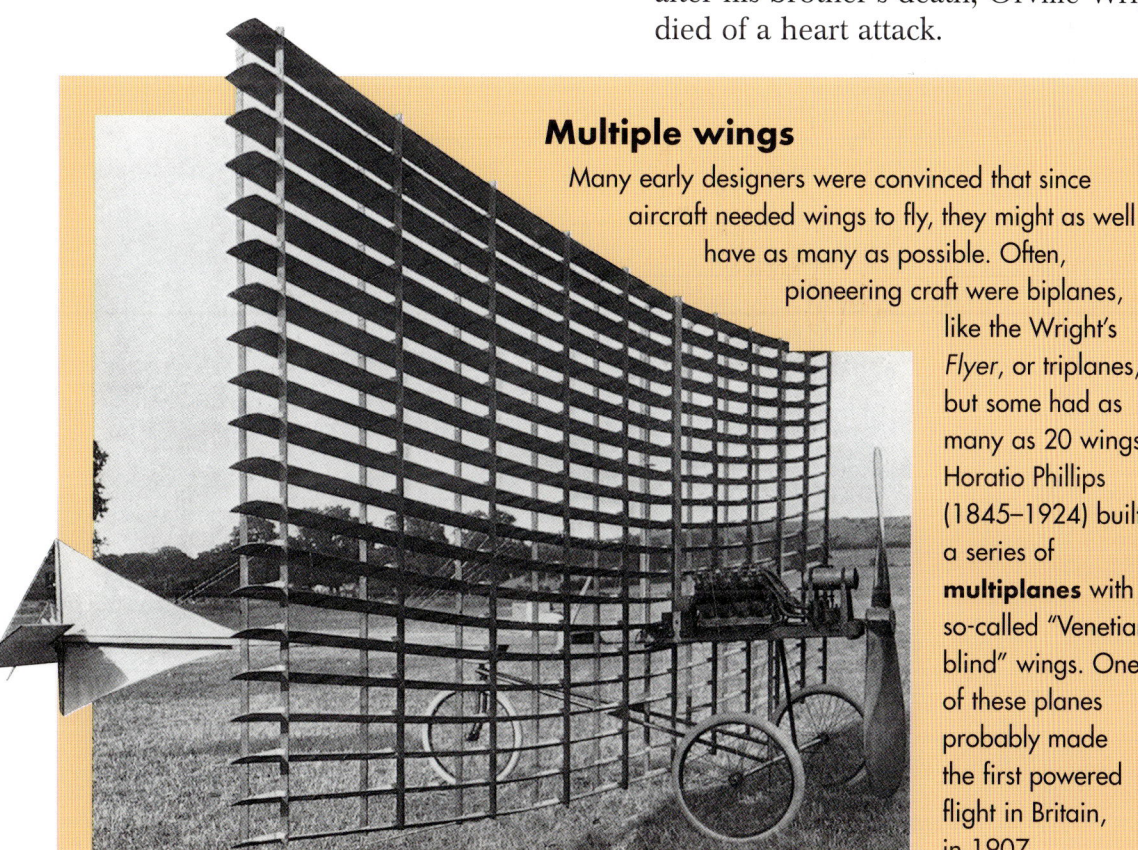

Multiple wings

Many early designers were convinced that since aircraft needed wings to fly, they might as well have as many as possible. Often, pioneering craft were biplanes, like the Wright's *Flyer*, or triplanes, but some had as many as 20 wings. Horatio Phillips (1845–1924) built a series of **multiplanes** with so-called "Venetian blind" wings. One of these planes probably made the first powered flight in Britain, in 1907.

Louis Blériot

1872–1936

Louis Blériot made the first international flight. He flew solo across the English Channel, from France to England, in 1909.

Blériot was born in the town of Cambrai, in northern France, and studied arts and trades in Paris. Around the turn of the twentieth century, when there were very few cars on the road, he designed and manufactured headlamps and other car accessories. These sold very well. At the same time, Blériot began experimenting with flying machines. In 1902, as the Wright brothers were developing their *Flyer*, he built a model **ornithopter**, which was designed to fly by flapping its wings.

From gliders to monoplanes

Like many other air pioneers, Blériot began by designing and building gliders. His first, in 1905, was towed along by a boat on the River Seine in Paris. Two years later, he built his first monoplane, which was unusual at the time because most aviators were more interested in multiplanes. Perhaps Blériot was the first to realize that a single wing was more efficient because air passed over it more smoothly. He added a small engine, which turned a propeller behind the wings in the same way as the Wrights' *Flyer*.

Louis Blériot was a successful aircraft designer and manufacturer, as well as a daring pilot.

LOUIS BLÉRIOT

Like all planes of the time, Blériot's Type XI had an open **cockpit**. It had a single propeller, powered by a motorcycle engine.

Crash landing

Blériot soon realized that his monoplane worked better with the propeller in front of the wings, and he redesigned it with the help of his friend Louis Peyret. His Type VI aircraft, which he called *Lillebule* (the French for "dragonfly"), had a sliding seat that the pilot used to help the plane climb and dive. In 1907, Blériot was flying *Lillebule* when his engine cut out and the aircraft plummeted. Blériot slid his seat back as far as he could but this was not enough, so he threw himself towards the tail of the plane. Just in time, *Lillebule* leveled out before hitting the ground. It crumpled in a heap, which was not surprising since its wing surfaces were paper! But Blériot walked away unhurt.

Gaining fame

The Reims **air show** of 1909 was the world's first international aviation meeting. Thirty-eight airplanes appeared at the meeting, although only 23 actually managed to leave the ground. Louis Blériot entered three different planes, and a Wright A plane was piloted by Count de Lambert. Demonstration flights (like this one over the English seashore) caused great public interest in flying.

Challenge of the Channel

Early in 1909, the London *Daily Mail* newspaper offered a prize of £1,000 (about $1,500) to the first person to fly across the English Channel in an airplane. Several challengers, including Count Charles de Lambert and Hubert Latham, tried to win the prize before Blériot – but they all failed. Latham made a gallant attempt on July 19, 1909, flying from the French side near Calais in his Antoinette IV aircraft. He was doing well until his engine failed and he was forced to ditch in the water. He was soon picked up by a French navy ship, but he had to wait for another Antoinette to be delivered before he could try again. Meanwhile, Blériot was almost ready to make his attempt.

Blériot takes off

On July 25, 1909 Blériot got up before dawn at Les Barraques, near Calais. His foot was hurting from a previous crash, but he went for a car drive and felt much better afterward. He rushed to his **hangar** and climbed aboard his Type XI monoplane, taking off from French soil at 4:41 A.M.. His wife, Alice, watched the flight from a French ship. Blériot headed across the Channel, flying at a height of between 165 ft and 330 ft and a speed of about 45 mph.

Blériot in his cockpit, which was very flimsy and provided little protection in the event of a crash. Later, in 1909, he had another crash. Once again he survived, but this time with injuries to his ribs and liver.

Historic flight

Blériot had no **compass** and tried to keep straight, but when at last the shore appeared, he realized that the wind had carried him to the east. Approaching the white cliffs of Dover, he turned west, flew in over an opening in the cliffs, cut his engine, and bumped down hard on the grass of Northfall Meadow near Dover Castle. It was 5:17 A.M., and Blériot had become the first person to fly across the English Channel.

Hubert Latham

Hubert Latham (1883–1918), born in France and educated in England, was Louis Blériot's great rival. Two days after Blériot won the *Daily Mail* prize, Latham tried again to cross the Channel. This time his engine failed when he was just about 1 mile from the English coast and once again he had to **ditch** in the water. The following month, the rivals met again at the Reims air show. There Latham had the satisfaction of breaking speed and **altitude** records.

Flying passengers, students, and mail

Within days of his cross-Channel flight, Blériot had taken more than a hundred orders for his Type XI plane. Later in the year, his Type XII was the first to fly with two passengers and he soon opened flying schools near Paris and London. One of his planes made the first non-stop flight between these two cities in 1911, as well as making the first airmail flights in England. During World War I, Blériot built planes for the French air force and after the war he turned to commercial aircraft. He remained active in the **aeronautics** industry until he died of a heart attack in 1936, at the age of 64.

Louis Blériot poses for the camera with his wife and well-wishers after his historic crossing of the English Channel.

Alcock and Brown

Sir John Alcock 1892–1919
Sir Arthur Whitten Brown 1886–1948

British aviators John Alcock and Arthur Whitten Brown were the first to fly non-stop across the Atlantic Ocean in 1919.

In 1913, the London *Daily Mail* offered a prize of £10,000 (about $15,000) for the first non-stop transatlantic flight. The following year, before anyone could think seriously about taking up the challenge, World War I broke out. When it was over, two airmen decided to take up the challenge.

In the Royal Naval Flying Service

John Alcock, the son of a Manchester horse dealer, first worked as an **apprentice** motor mechanic. At the age of 18, he changed to airplanes, which he tuned before he gained his pilot's certificate. Alcock joined the Royal Naval Flying Service (RNFS) in 1914 as an instructor before becoming a flight sub-lieutenant. In 1917, he fought enemy **seaplanes** in his Sopwith Camel, which earned him the Distinguished Service Cross. Alcock was captured by the Turks after he was forced to ditch his aircraft in the Mediterranean Sea, and he remained a prisoner until the end of the war. He left the RNFS determined to attempt a flight across the Atlantic.

Captain Alcock (top) and Lieutenant Brown both had plenty of flying experience. Alcock piloted their plane on its famous trip across the Atlantic.

ALCOCK AND BROWN

World War I

When war broke out in 1914, military leaders realized that these new airplanes could be very useful. At first, planes were mainly used for watching the movement of enemy forces. Then, as planes got sturdier and engines more powerful, they became fighters and bombers. Faster aircraft were developed, and by 1918 they could fly twice as fast as they could at the beginning of the war.

In the Royal Flying Corps

Arthur Whitten Brown was born in Glasgow, the only son of American parents. In 1914, he joined the Royal Flying Corps, where he trained as an **observer**. He was shot-down over enemy territory in 1915 and remained a prisoner-of-war until 1917. He then worked for the government in aircraft production and gained a private pilot's licence. At the end of the war, the Royal Naval Flying Service and the Royal Flying Corps merged to form the Royal Air Force (RAF). In 1919 Brown was delighted when John Alcock asked him to be his **navigator**.

Take-off from North America

Alcock approached Vickers Aeroplanes who agreed that he could make his attempt in a Vickers Vimy bomber. The plane was shipped to St. Johns, on the east coast of Newfoundland (now part of Canada). From the spring of 1919, twelve crews had assembled there to try for the prize.

Ready to try

In May, one crew had to make a forced landing halfway across the ocean and another crashed on take-off. On June 14, Alcock and Brown were ready to try. Their Vickers Vimy had extra fuel tanks fitted, making it very heavy. The twin Rolls Royce Eagle engines roared as the plane tried to get airborne. At 16:13 **GMT** it lifted off.

This Curtiss NC–4 flying boat flew across the Atlantic a few weeks before Alcock and Brown, but put down on the sea along the way.

Over the Atlantic

The propeller that drove the Vimy's wireless **generator** broke off ten minutes after take-off, and later the airspeed indicator failed, making both flying and navigating more difficult. Alcock and Brown were soon flying between a bank of clouds and thick fog. After some hours, the cloud cover cleared and Brown was able to use the stars and moon to check their position. When the clouds returned, the plane suddenly went into a spin and dived down from 4,000 ft.

Dangerous moments

The plane was very close to the water when Alcock managed to regain control. They climbed again, only to be met in their open cockpit with hail and sleet, which iced-up the engine radiators and the fuel gauge. Brown had to climb out of his seat to clear them.

Soft landing

They were flying through low cloud and rain when they crossed the west coast of Ireland. At 8:40 A.M. they landed at Clifden, on what turned out to be a peat bog. This was land, but it was not very dry. By the time the Vimy came to a standstill, it was nose-down in the bog. Fortunately, there was little damage and the two freezing airmen were delighted. They had flown 1,900 miles in 16 hours and 27 minutes – and had crossed the Atlantic non-stop.

It was a difficult landing – but they made it!

ALCOCK AND BROWN

Britain to Australia

Five months after Alcock and Brown's transatlantic flight, two Australian brothers flew halfway around the world in another Vickers Vimy. Captain Ross Smith and Lieutenant Keith Smith won the London-to-Australia Air Derby. They took 28 days to fly over 11,250 miles to Darwin, with many stops across Europe and Asia on the way. The brothers shared the £10,000 (about $15,000) prize offered by the Australian government.

Knights of the British Empire

Six days later, the two men were received by King George V at Windsor Castle, where they were **knighted**. Sadly, Sir John Alcock was killed later that year when his Vickers Viking crashed in France. Sir Arthur Whitten Brown went on to work for Vickers. During World War II, he went back into the RAF to train pilots in navigation and engineering. His only son was killed in action with the RAF in 1944, and Sir Arthur died four years later.

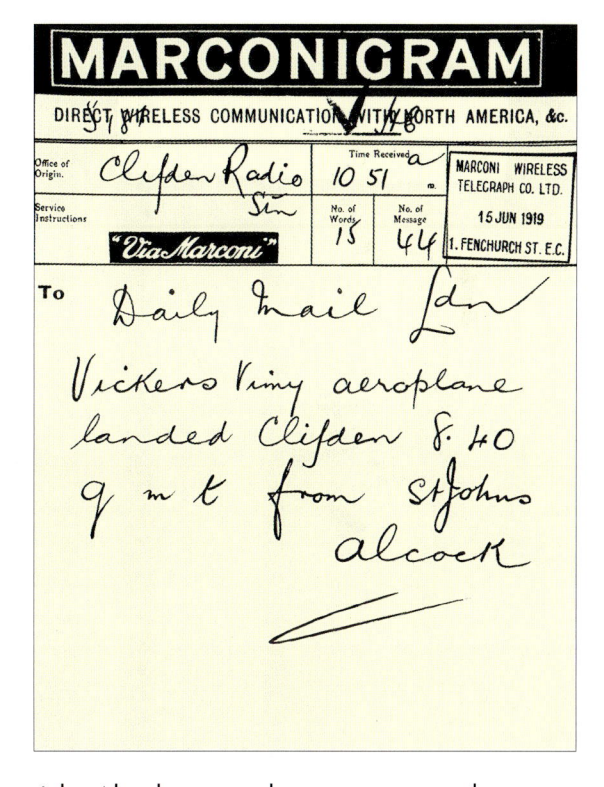

John Alcock sent a telegram at once to the sponsors of the prize.

Charles Lindbergh

1902–1974

American aviator Charles Lindbergh is best known for making the first solo flight across the Atlantic, from New York to Paris, in 1927.

In 1919, the same year in which Alcock and Brown first flew the Atlantic, a French-born hotelier named Raymond B. Orteig offered a prize of $25,000 for the first pilot to fly non-stop from New York to Paris. During the early 1920s, several pilots tried to win the prize, but they all failed and some were killed in the attempt. In 1926, an American airmail pilot named Charles Lindbergh decided that it was his turn to try.

Longing to fly

Charles Lindbergh was born in Detroit, Michigan, but the family soon moved to Minnesota where his father practiced law and was elected a member of **Congress**. The young Charles was fascinated by machinery, especially cars and motorcycles. He first drove the family Model T Ford at the age of 11. When he was 16, he took over the family farm, and four years later went to study **mechanical engineering** at the University of Wisconsin. By this time, however, he was itching to fly, and in 1922 he left college to go to flying school in Nebraska.

Charles Lindbergh became a celebrity and spread the popularity of flying.

CHARLES LINDBERGH

Airmail
The idea of being able to deliver mail speedily also helped the development of aviation. Official airmail deliveries began as early as 1911 in both Britain and the U.S., and the first airmail planes were Blériot monoplanes. In 1919, William Boeing's company started an airmail service between the U.S. and Canada, and this gave the opportunity for many pilots such as Charles Lindbergh to find work.

"Lucky Lindy"
In 1925, Lindbergh became a captain in the U.S. Air Service Reserve. While practising a surprise attack, his plane was hit by another. Both airmen **bailed out** and parachuted safely to the ground. Perhaps this gave birth to Lindbergh's nickname "Lucky Lindy." He later became a pilot for the Air Mail Service. It was then that Lindbergh heard about the Orteig prize.

Lindbergh on his historic flight. His Ryan NYP plane had very poor forward vision.

Taking up the NYP challenge
Lindbergh's plane was a Ryan NYP (New York to Paris) high-wing monoplane, which he named the *Spirit of St. Louis*. It had a Wright Whirlwind engine and was fitted with extra fuel tanks. These were so big that the plane had a **periscope** allowing the pilot to see straight ahead. Otherwise, Lindbergh just had to look out of the side windows. At last everything was ready, and he took off in mist and rain from Long Island, New York at 7:52 A.M. on May 20, 1927.

The long flight

As he had not slept for 36 hours before take-off, Lindbergh's biggest battle was overcoming tiredness. He flew over Newfoundland and then headed across the Atlantic Ocean to Ireland. Ice on the wings was a hazard and at one time fog forced him to fly very low over the waves. Lindbergh flew on over Cornwall and the English Channel, and finally landed at Le Bourget, Paris, at 10:24 P.M. on May 21. There the darkness was lit up by the headlamps of hundreds of cars of people who had driven there to greet him. The flight had taken 33 hours and covered 3,630 miles. Captain Lindbergh was the ninety-second person to cross the Atlantic by air, but the first to do so alone.

Flying stardom

People all over the world read about this epic flight in their newspapers. In 1929, Lindbergh married Anne Morrow, daughter of the U.S. Ambassador to Mexico. He taught her to fly and she was his **co-pilot** on many flights, including an **intercontinental** journey from Washington to Tokyo.

Mr. and Mrs. Lindbergh, pilot and co-pilot, in 1930.

Family tragedy

In 1932, tragedy struck the Lindberghs. One night their two-year-old son was kidnapped from their home in New Jersey and murdered. There was a great deal of publicity about the case, which led to a new "Lindbergh law" that made kidnapping a crime punishable by death. In 1936, a man was convicted of the murder and executed.

World War II and after

After being invited to visit German airfields and factories, Lindbergh was awarded a medal, the German Eagle with Star. It was presented to him by Hermann Goering, a high ranking Nazi official. This caused an outcry in America among critics of Nazi Germany, especially after Lindbergh suggested that the U.S. should not get involved in World War II. However, when the U.S. entered the war, Lindbergh did all he could as a civilian. He served as a consultant to the United Aircraft Corporation and flew combat missions in the Pacific. This restored the reputation of "Lucky Lindy." He died of natural causes in Hawaii in 1974.

President Franklin D. Roosevelt (1882–1945) was outraged by some of Lindbergh's public statements.

Pulitzer Prize winner

Lindbergh described his historic flight in a book called *The Spirit of St. Louis*, published in 1953. This won a Pulitzer Prize, an annual award for literature. Four years later, it was made into a film by Billy Wilder, starring James Stewart. Books and films such as these also helped make flying more popular at a time when most long journeys were still being made by rail or by sea.

Amelia Earhart

1897–1937

American aviator Amelia Earhart broke many flying records. She became a worldwide celebrity and paved the way for many other women pilots.

In the early days of aviation, there were very few women pilots. Since flying was daring and dangerous, many people believed that it was not suitable for women. Amelia Earhart was one of the few exceptions. Born a few years before the first powered flights, she came to love planes and went on to become a true pioneer and heroine. Her exploits fascinated people around the world, but today she is most famous for her mysterious disappearance.

Growing up

Amelia Earhart was born in 1897 in the small town of Atchison, Kansas. She had a younger sister called Muriel and the two girls were very close. In 1904, Edwin Earhart, who was a lawyer, took his daughters to the World's Fair in St. Louis. Earhart loved the roller coaster and other hair-raising rides. At home, she liked horse riding, and her favorite book was *Black Beauty*. Eventually, the two girls were sent away to school – Amelia to Pennsylvania, and Muriel to Canada. In 1918, Amelia went to Toronto and became a nurse in a military hospital.

Amelia Earhart became the most famous woman pilot, known all around the world.

AMELIA EARHART

Catching the flying bug

In 1919, Amelia began studying medicine in New York, but then her parents asked her to join them in California. There her father took her to an air display and Amelia was taken up for a ten-minute flight. She later wrote: "As soon as we left the ground I knew myself I had to fly,"

Determined to fly

Amelia begged her father to allow her to learn to fly. When she found a female pilot to teach her, her father gave in. Once she could fly, Amelia wanted her own plane and she did many jobs to pay for it. She worked in her father's firm, in a telephone office, as a photographer, and even as a truckdriver.

Amelia Earhart with pilot A. N. White at Northolt Airport, near London, in 1928.

The Ninety-Nines

In 1929, a group of women pilots decided it would be a good idea to form a club to further their cause. They gathered together in Long Island, New York and thought about a name for the club. They considered the names "Angels' Club" and "Bird Women," but finally decided on the number of members they thought they could find. And so the Ninety-Nines Club was born, with Amelia Earhart as its first president. She later wrote: "Women must try to do things as men have tried. When they fail, their failure must be but a challenge to others."

Amelia Earhart with navigator Fred Noonan. On their final flight, they both disappeared without trace.

Breaking records

In 1922, Earhart broke her first record, taking the women's altitude mark up to 14,224 ft. She moved to Boston and went on flying. Like everyone else, she was very excited when Charles Lindbergh flew across the Atlantic. The following year, she became the first woman to make a transatlantic flight, as part of a three-person crew. Though she took a turn at the controls, Earhart was basically a passenger – but it would not be long before she flew across the Atlantic on her own.

The Atlantic again

In 1931, Earhart married the publisher George Putnam, who had helped her with her first book. Together they planned the trip that made her even more famous. On May 20, 1932 at 7:12 P.M., she took off in her Lockheed Vega from Newfoundland and the next day at 1:45 P.M. she touched down near the village of Culmore, in Northern Ireland. This was the first **solo** crossing of the Atlantic by a woman and it created a sensation. Earhart received telegrams of congratulation from US President Herbert Hoover, British Prime Minister Ramsay MacDonald, and Charles Lindbergh.

Amelia Earhart climbs down from her plane after flying across the Atlantic Ocean.

Attempt to conquer the world

Further successful long-distance flights, such as from Hawaii to California in 1935, made Earhart think about a round-the-world trip. She decided to fly east from the United States, roughly along the Equator all the way around the globe, with as few stops as possible on the way. An experienced navigator, Fred Noonan, was hired to fly with her in a Lockheed Electra. On June 1, 1937, they took off from Miami, heading for South America and then Africa. They flew on to South east Asia, where they were delayed by bad weather. By June 29, they had arrived in New Guinea. On the next leg they would fly to tiny Howland Island, more than 2,500 miles away.

Radio silence

On July 2 the Electra took off from Lae, New Guinea. For the first few hours the plane was in radio contact with Lae, and then with an American ship positioned near Howland Island. Earhart reported that they were on course, but after more than 19 hours of flying she said that they must be near, but could not see, the island. She also reported that fuel was running low. The airfield at Howland was ready to receive the Electra but the plane never arrived. Navy ships and aircraft combed the region for weeks, but no trace of Earhart or her plane were ever found. Amelia Earhart and her navigator were never seen again.

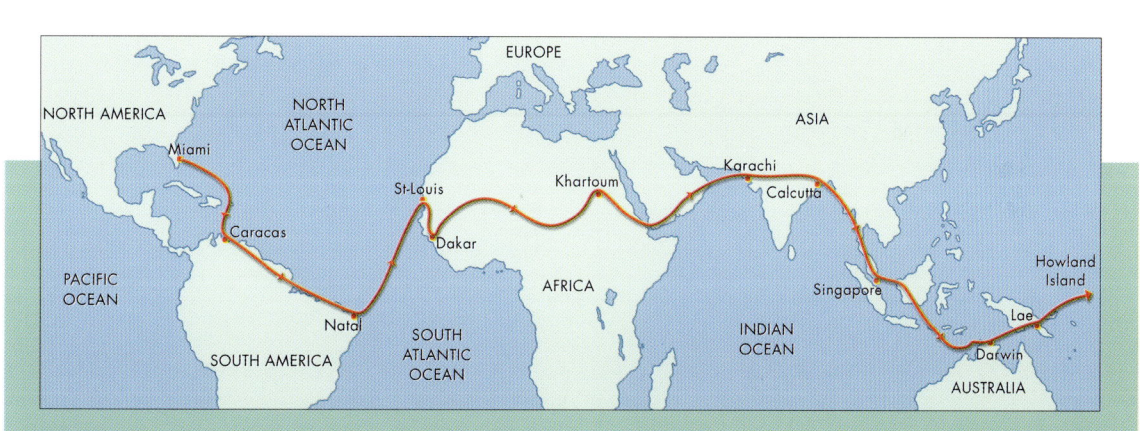

Mysterious disappearance

Most people believe that Amelia Earhart's Electra was blown off course on its way to Howland Island before crashing and sinking (the map above shows her route). But other theories have been put forward to solve the mystery of Amelia Earhart's disappearance. Some say she was spying for the United States and was captured on Japanese territory. Others think that the plane crashed on an uninhabited island and Amelia and Fred lived there for years. Special projects still exist to try to solve the mystery.

Amy Johnson

1903-1941

Amy Johnson was a famous British airwoman. She set several long-distance flying records and helped further the cause of women's flying.

Amy Johnson was born in the fishing port of Kingston-upon-Hull, on the Yorkshire coast. Her grandfather was a Dane who had sailed to Hull at the age of 16 and changed his name from Jorgensen to Johnson. Amy was the eldest daughter of John, a herring importer, and his wife Amy. The young Johnson lived at home in Hull until she went to college in Sheffield, where she gained her degree in 1925. She then moved to London, where she worked as a secretary in a firm of lawyers. It was in London that she took up a hobby that would become a passion for the rest of her short life – flying.

Ground engineer

Johnson was fascinated by mechanical things and she started to spend most of her spare time at the London Aeroplane Club. She decided to train for a ground engineer's license, which she gained in 1929, along with a full navigation certificate. For a while, she was the only female ground engineer in the world. But she soon took to the air, deciding that she wanted to show that women could be just as good aviators as men.

Amy Johnson's signed photograph became a very popular memento.

AMY JOHNSON

Gipsy Moth

The first de Havilland DH60 ("Moth") biplane was produced in Britain in 1925. Three years later, a more powerful 100-horsepower Gipsy engine was added. The so-called Gipsy Moth was sturdy and reliable, with a wood and fabric structure and a strong undercarriage. This made it popular with long-distance pilots and many flying clubs ordered Moths. More than 1,000 were built, and some **renovated** models are still flying today. Amy Johnson's *Jason* is in the Science Museum in London, England.

Challenge

Johnson's first challenge was to become the first woman to fly from Europe to Australia. But first she needed a plane, so she had to look around for financial backing. Eventually, her father helped her buy a second-hand Gipsy Moth, which she named *Jason* after the trademark of her father's firm.

Take-off

She took-off from Croydon Airport on May 5, 1930. On the first day she was almost overcome by fuel fumes before landing in Vienna. Then a sandstorm forced her to make an emergency landing in the desert near Baghdad, Iraq, where she had to use a rifle to frighten off wild dogs. At last she arrived in Karachi, in present-day Pakistan, ahead of schedule.

Amy Johnson leaves London for Australia. As well as becoming the first woman to fly to Australia, she also wanted to beat Bert Hinkler's record of 16 days for the flight, set in 1928.

Bumpy landing

Flying on from Karachi, she landed by mistake on a college sports field in Burma (Myanmar). The bumpy landing caused damage to a wing, which students helped her repair. A fire engine then carried her plane to a safe launch site, but this all meant that she lost valuable time.

On to Darwin

On the island of Timor, Johnson landed in a field that turned out to be full of huge termite mounds. Locals had to help her clear a flat runway. Finally, she arrived in Darwin on the north coast of Australia on May 24. There she received a tremendous welcome, but Johnson was disappointed that she had missed breaking the time record by three days.

Amy Johnson in Darwin. She was the first woman to fly solo from Europe to Australia.

Record-breaker

Amy Johnson went on to beat many other records. In 1931, she flew *Jason II* from England to Japan in less than nine days, with a total flying time of 79 hours. The following year she married a rival, the pilot Jim Mollison, and less than four months later she beat one of the records held by her new husband. She flew solo from England to Cape Town, South Africa, in just over four days. She then took to flying with her husband and together they broke more speed and distance records.

AMY JOHNSON

Queen of the Air

After her England–Australia flight in 1930, Amy Johnson was known as the "Queen of the Air," and some newspapers referred to her as the "darling of the people." Songs and poems were written about "Johnnie from the blue," including this piece of music. Many people did not realise how inexperienced Johnson was as a pilot. Later, she wrote about her Australian flight: "The prospect did not frighten me, because I was so appallingly ignorant that I never realised in the least what I had taken on." She was very modest. When she saw that huge crowds had turned out to see her return to London, she said that people must be sick of hearing about her. They certainly weren't!

The Air Transport Auxiliary

When war broke out in 1939, Johnson joined the Air Transport Auxiliary, which flew airplanes from factories to RAF bases throughout Britain. She must have enjoyed working alongside her male and female colleagues in such an important job. On one such flight in January 1941, however, the Airspeed Oxford that Johnson was piloting ran out of fuel and crashed into the freezing waters of the Thames estuary. Amy Johnson was just 37 when she died.

Amy Johnson and her husband in Wales in 1933, before their non-stop flight to the U.S.

IGOR SIKORSKY

1889–1972

Igor Sikorsky was a pioneer in aircraft design, who is best known for his successful development of the helicopter.

Sikorsky was just 14 when the Wright brothers made their first flight, and six years later he was working on his first helicopter. Yet it took another 30 years to perfect this idea, by which time Russian-born Sikorsky was an American citizen and had already designed the world's first **multi-engined** airplane. By the time he died at the age of 83, jet airliners were flying passengers all over the world and helicopters had found their own unique flying role.

Flying straight up

Sikorsky was born in 1889 in Kiev, the capital of modern Ukraine, then an important city in Imperial Russia. His father was a psychology professor and his mother a medical school graduate. Igor, the youngest of five children, was interested in science and engineering from an early age. In 1903, he entered the Russian Naval Academy and four years later transferred to the Polytechnic Institute. By now he was tinkering with ideas for flying machines. After a visit to Paris, Sikorsky decided that the way to fly was straight up, like a "flying windmill."

Aircraft designer Igor Sikorsky emigrated to the United States at the age of 29.

IGOR SIKORSKY

Whirlybird

Around the year 1500, the great Italian artist, inventor, and scientist Leonardo da Vinci (1452–1519) drew designs for several flying machines. One, in particular, struck the young Igor when he saw it. This was a machine called a helixpteron (or "spiral wing"), which had a large rotating screw on top. Leonardo's ideas were brilliant, but he was never able to put them into practice.

First attempts

In 1909, Sikorsky fitted a small engine to his first helicopters but they failed to lift off. He decided to work on a fixed-wing biplane instead, and his S–2 carried him on his first short flight. By 1911, his S–5 stayed in the air for more than an hour and made cross-country flights. During one test flight the engine failed, and Sikorsky had to make a forced landing. He saw that a mosquito drawn into the engine had caused the problem. This led him to develop a plane with several engines, which made it much safer.

Four engines

While working at the Russo-Baltic Railroad Car Works in St. Petersburg, Sikorsky developed the world's first four-engined airplane in 1913. Called *Le Grand*, it had an enclosed cabin for pilots and passengers and became the model for later planes. Sikorsky insisted on piloting his own planes first, and he soon made a flight of almost two hours. Tsar Nicholas II inspected the plane and rewarded its designer with a gold watch inscribed with the Russian imperial eagle.

Sikorsky's huge *Le Grand* biplane.

Emigration to America

After the Russian Revolution of 1917, Sikorsky saw little hope of further aircraft development at home or in Europe. He decided to **emigrate** to the United States and in 1919 sailed to New York. He worked as a lecturer and school teacher for a few years, and then set up his own aircraft company in an old barn near Roosevelt Field, Long Island. In 1928, he became a U.S. citizen and the following year his company joined the United Aircraft Corporation. In 1931, Sikorsky designed the S–40 American Clipper flying boat for the new company. By 1937, these four-engined planes were flying across the Atlantic and Pacific oceans for Pan American Airways.

Back to the helicopter

Thirty years after his first attempts, Sikorsky returned to work on the development of his helicopter. Other designers and inventors had made progress, but Sikorsky wanted to produce a really practical machine. His VS–300 lifted off on September 14, 1939, with its designer at the controls. Sikorsky wrote later: "I have never been in the air in a machine that was as pleasant to fly as the helicopter." In 1941, the VS-300 set a new record for a helicopter by staying airborne for one-and-a-half hours. His original Russian dream had become an American reality.

Sikorsky at the flying controls of his revolutionary VS-300 helicopter.

IGOR SIKORSKY

Bigger and faster

In 1947, Los Angeles Airways launched the world's first helicopter mail service with a fleet of Sikorsky S-51s. By the time he retired from his own company in 1957, Sikorsky had seen his helicopters grow in size and power. This development continued during his retirement. In 1965, a Sikorsky SH–3A Sea King made the first non-stop helicopter flight across the North American continent – and in 1967 two Sikorsky HH–3s flew from New York to Paris. Igor Sikorsky carried on working as a consultant to his company until his death in 1972.

Several engineers work at the same time on a Sikorsky production line. Igor Sikorsky introduced the first helicopter production line in 1944, at his factory in Bridgeport, Connecticut.

Air rescue

Sikorsky realized that helicopters were the most versatile of aircraft as they can **hover** in one place and are ideal for rescue missions. The first took place in 1944, when a Sikorsky helicopter rushed from New York to help the victims of a steamship explosion. Today, choppers are used for dramatic rescues, such as lifting sailors from sinking ships, saving climbers trapped on cliffs and mountains, or rescuing people cut off by floods, fires, and other natural disasters. They are also used by the emergency services as air ambulances.

Frank Whittle

1907–1996

Sir Frank Whittle was a British aviation engineer who invented the jet engine.

Until the 1940s, all aircraft were powered by **piston engines** that turned propellers. By then engineers had already realized that they needed a new form of power if they wanted to make aircraft go faster. One way was to send them up higher, where air resistance is less. But piston engines and propellers do not work well in the thinner air that is found at high altitudes. So the answer had to be a completely different kind of engine. Frank Whittle first suggested his revolutionary idea in 1928, but it was many years before the world's first jet aircraft took off.

Model airplanes

Frank Whittle was born in Coventry in England where his father ran an engineering business. He was interested in mechanical things at a very young age and enjoyed playing with model airplanes. Flying was still in its very early years but young Frank was fascinated by aviation.

Sir Frank Whittle's invention of the jet engine changed the world of aviation.

FRANK WHITTLE 39

The race for jet supremacy

In Germany, Hans Pabst von Ohain (1911–1998) began working on a jet engine in 1936 at the Heinkel aircraft factory. He also ran a ground test in 1937, after Whittle's, but the Germans took less time to produce their first jet aircraft. The Heinkel He 178 took off just a week before the start of World War II in 1939, but it was not until 1944 that the first jet aircraft went into full military service. This was the twin-engined Messerschmitt Me 262 (right).

RAF Cadet

Whittle left school at the age of 16 and joined the Royal Air Force as an apprentice **fitter**. There he soon designed his own model planes and was selected to become a **cadet** and train as a pilot. He went to the RAF College at Cranwell, and at the age of 21 wrote a thesis on "Future Developments in Aircraft Design." In this thesis, he first suggested the idea of **jet propulsion**.

The former Princess Elizabeth (now Queen Elizabeth II) inspecting cadets at the Royal Air Force College, Cranwell, in Lincolnshire, England.

The jet engine

Jet engines (like the one being inspected by Sir Frank Whittle, left) are simpler than piston engines, but they use a lot of fuel. They work by the same reaction force that makes an air-filled balloon zoom through the air when you let it go. The engine sucks in air at the front and then **compresses** it. This compressed air is then sprayed with fuel and the mixture is lit by an electric spark. The burning gases expand and blast out through the back of the engine. As the gases shoot backward, the engine and its aircraft are thrust forward.

Developing the idea

Whittle became a pilot officer in No. 111 Fighter **Squadron** and went on to become an instructor and then a **test pilot**. He mainly worked on seaplanes, but at the same time he continued to develop his jet ideas. He took out his first patent on a jet engine in 1930. Four years later he went to Cambridge University to study for a degree in mechanical sciences. Up to this time no one had shown any great interest in his ideas, but in Cambridge two former RAF officers encouraged Whittle to carry on his revolutionary work. They formed a small company called Power Jets, and Whittle began work on an experimental engine. On April 12, 1937 Whittle tested his first engine, codenamed W.1, on the ground, to see if it would work properly. In fact, it ran very well indeed.

The first successful jet engine

According to Whittle, the engine – the first successful jet engine in the world – "made a noise like an air-raid siren." The British Air Ministry, which had shown little interest before, now saw its potential and soon placed a contract for a Whittle engine so that it could be tested in an aircraft. At last, Whittle had the backing he needed and the race towards the jet age was on.

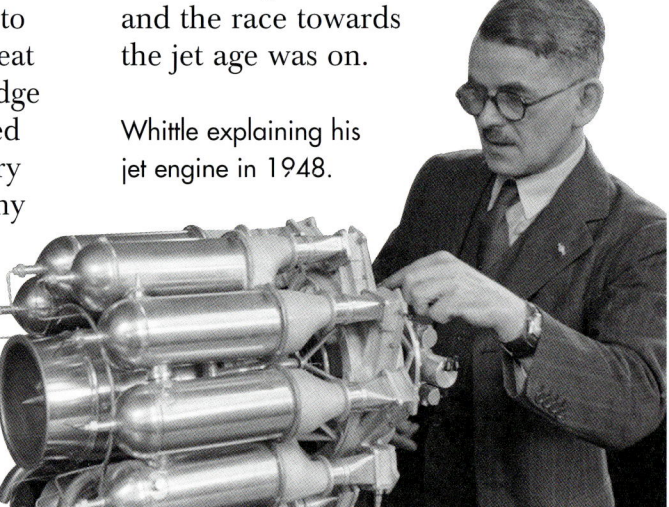

Whittle explaining his jet engine in 1948.

FRANK WHITTLE

The Gloster Meteor was one of the most successful early jet aircraft.

The Gloster Meteor

The Gloster Aircraft Company was given the task of building the first British jet aircraft. Meanwhile, Whittle and 40 workers continued to test and perfect the W.1 engine. On May 15, 1941, Flight Lieutenant Gerry Sayer took off from Cranwell in a Gloster E.28/39, powered by Whittle's engine. The flight lasted 17 minutes, and this and further trial flights were a great success. Further developments on both the aircraft and the engine led to the Gloster Meteor entering service with the RAF in July 1944. The new technology meant that this jet fighter could fly at 423 mph at a height of over 30,000 ft. By 1946, a Meteor F4 has broken the world air speed record, flying at 620 mph.

Air commodore

In 1944, Whittle's company was taken over by the British government. Before the end of the war, Whittle was promoted to the rank of air commodore. He was knighted by King George VI in 1948 and retired from the RAF in the same year. He become a consultant for various companies, including the British Overseas Airways Corporation (now British Airways). In 1950, he was invited on board a Vickers Viscount that flew from London to Paris on the world's first jet-powered passenger service. His invention had come a long way!

Research in the U.S.

Whittle moved to the U.S. in 1976 and became a research professor at the U.S. Naval Academy in Maryland. He died in America of cancer in 1996, aged 89.

CHUCK YEAGER

1923- Charles ("Chuck") Yeager was the first man to fly faster than the speed of sound.

By the mid-1940s, the new jet planes were flying close to the speed of sound (around 762 mph). As they got near this speed, pilots felt their planes being buffeted, as if they were coming up against a "sound barrier." These effects were caused by increased **turbulence** in the air flowing past the wings and **fuselage**, but could a plane fly through this "barrier?" Scientists and aviators were very keen to find out. In 1947, an American rocket-powered plane flown by test pilot Charles ("Chuck") Yeager gave them the answer.

Learning to fly

Chuck Yeager was born in Myra, West Virginia and grew up in the nearby village of Hamlin. His father was a gas-well driller. After leaving high school in 1941, Yeager joined the Army Air Corps, just three months before the United States entered World War II. After working briefly as an aircraft mechanic, he trained as a pilot and became a flight officer early in 1943. Later that year his fighter squadron was sent to Britain and soon Yeager was flying a P51 Mustang on combat missions against Germany.

U.S. Air Force officer and test pilot Chuck Yeager broke the sound barrier in 1947.

CHUCK YEAGER

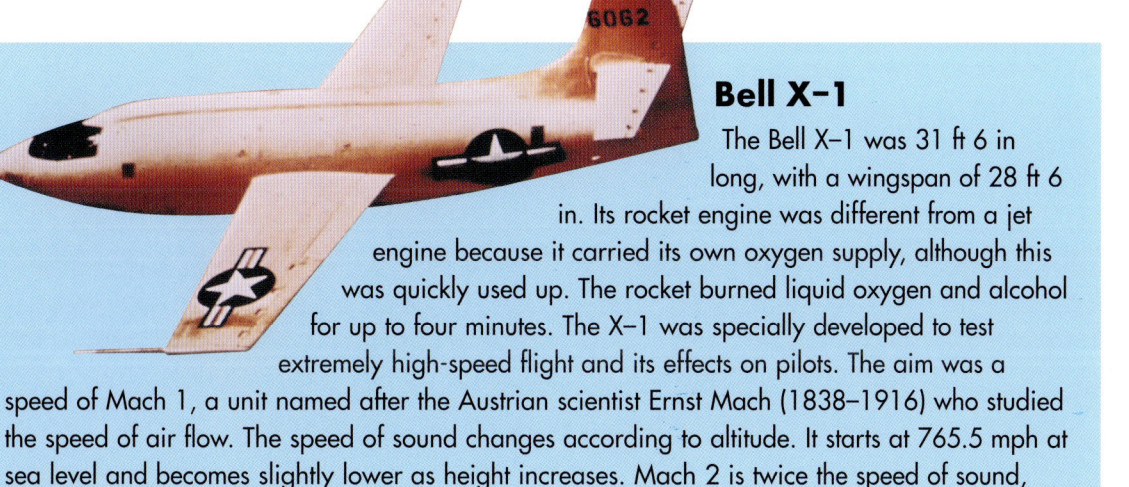

Bell X-1

The Bell X-1 was 31 ft 6 in long, with a wingspan of 28 ft 6 in. Its rocket engine was different from a jet engine because it carried its own oxygen supply, although this was quickly used up. The rocket burned liquid oxygen and alcohol for up to four minutes. The X-1 was specially developed to test extremely high-speed flight and its effects on pilots. The aim was a speed of Mach 1, a unit named after the Austrian scientist Ernst Mach (1838–1916) who studied the speed of air flow. The speed of sound changes according to altitude. It starts at 765.5 mph at sea level and becomes slightly lower as height increases. Mach 2 is twice the speed of sound, Mach 3 three times, and so on.

Shot down

On March 5, 1944, Yeager's plane was shot-down over German-occupied France. He was taken by members of the French underground movement across the Pyrenees Mountains to Spain, but there he was put in prison. He escaped and was helped back to Britain by the RAF. After returning to action, he won the Distinguished Flying Cross and several other military honors.

Test pilot

After the war Yeager returned to the U.S. to work as a flight instructor and then as a test pilot. He became a U.S.A.F. captain in 1947 and was selected as a test pilot for special research flights, including the secret, rocket-powered Bell X-1 plane which was being developed to fly at **supersonic** speeds. The tests were to be made over Rogers Dry Lake on the edge of the Mojave desert in California. Yeager first made some gliding flights and then used rocket power to get close to the speed of sound.

A P51 Mustang is cleared for take-off. In late 1944, Yeager was flying a Mustang when he downed a Messerschmitt Me 262 (see page 39).

Breaking the sound barrier

On October 14, 1947, the X-1 was carried up to 26,330 ft by a huge Boeing B-29 Superfortress. The B-29 then dived fast before releasing the X-1, with Captain Yeager at the controls. The small plane rocketed away and increased speed as it climbed steeply to 40,700 ft. The speed needle quickly approached Mach 1, the speed of sound, which at that altitude is around 666 mph. Then Yeager saw that he was flying at a supersonic Mach 1.06. He slowed down as the rocket fuel was almost used up and then took more than seven minutes to glide back to Earth. This flight proved that the sound barrier could be broken safely.

Yeager in the cockpit at Edwards Air Force Base in 1953.

Showing the world

As the tests were secret, news of the historic flight was only released the following year. Yeager went on testing new versions of the Bell research plane and in 1953 he piloted the X-1A to a record 1,662 mph – well over twice the speed of sound. During that flight, the rocket plane suddenly went out of control and dropped many thousands of yards before Yeager was able to regain control and land safely. By then, he was such an experienced pilot that he was asked to report on nearly every new aircraft that was being considered by the U.S. Air Force. During one of his busiest periods, he flew 27 different types of plane in one month.

Commemorative stamp

In 1997, Yeager celebrated the fiftieth anniversary of his X–1 flight by breaking the sound barrier in an F-15 fighter. A commemorative stamp was also issued to mark the occasion.

Further assignments

In 1954, Yeager returned to Europe to command a fighter squadron. He then went on to train pilots to become astronauts for the American space program before running the Aerospace Research Pilot School. There were many further military posts and missions before he retired from the U.S. Air Force in 1975, with the rank of brigadier general. He continued to serve as a test pilot.

The Bell X-1A that Yeager flew at record speeds in 1953.

Into the Hall of Fame

In 1973, Chuck Yeager was elected to the U.S. National Aviation Hall of Fame in Dayton, Ohio. Three years later President Gerald Ford presented him with a Congressional Medal of Honor for "advancing aerospace science a quantum step by proving that an aircraft could be flown at supersonic speeds." In 1983, Tom Wolfe's book about Chuck Yeager and the birth of the space program, called *The Right Stuff*, was made into a film.

GLOSSARY

Aeronautics The science and practice of flying.

Airborne In the air.

Airship A large balloon, often cigar-shaped, that can be steered and carries passengers.

Air show An exhibition of aircraft and flying displays.

Altitude Height in the air.

Apprentice A person who is learning a trade.

Aviation Flying in planes.

Aviator The pilot or flyer of a plane.

Bail out Make an emergency parachute jump from a plane.

Baronet A British noble title passed on in a family.

Biplane A plane with two sets of wings, one above the other.

Cadet A young person having training.

Cockpit The compartment of a plane where the pilot sits.

Compass An instrument that can show direction.

Compress To squeeze and increase the pressure of air.

Congress The group of elected representatives that makes laws in the United States.

Co-pilot A second pilot in an aircraft.

Ditch Bring an aircraft down on the sea in an emergency.

Emigrate To move to a new country.

Fitter A kind of mechanic.

Fuselage The main body of an aircraft.

Generator A machine that can make electricity.

Glider A plane that flies without the use of an engine.

GMT Greenwich Mean Time.

Hangar A building where aircraft are kept.

Hover To stay in one place in the air.

Hydrogen A light gas.

Intercontinental Between continents.

Jet propulsion Movement driven by a jet engine.

GLOSSARY

Knighted Given the title "Sir" by a British king or queen.

Mechanical engineering The branch of engineering that deals with the design and construction of machines.

Member of Parliament A person elected to represent people in the British government.

Monoplane A plane with one set of wings.

Multi-engined With several engines.

Multiplane A plane with several sets of wings.

Navigation Finding the way by following a course.

Navigator A crew member who directs the course of an aircraft.

Observer A person carried in a plane to watch the enemy's position.

Ornithopter A machine that flies by flapping wings.

Patent A document giving a person the individual right to an invention.

Periscope An apparatus that helps people see over an obstruction.

Physicist A scientist who studies matter and energy.

Piston A fitting that moves up and down in an engine to make other parts move.

Piston engine An engine in which pistons are moved by burning fuel, as in planes and cars.

Propeller A set of turning blades, driven by an engine, that push a plane through the air.

Renovate Restore to good condition.

Seaplane A plane designed to take off from and come down on water.

Solo Alone; on one's own.

Squadron A unit or group of military aircraft.

Supersonic Flying faster than the speed of sound.

Test pilot A pilot who flies new aircraft to test them.

Triplane A plane with three sets of wings, one above the other.

Turbulence An irregular or disturbed flow of air.

Undercarriage A set of wheels under an aircraft that support it on the ground.

INDEX

aerial carriage 8
Aerodrome 11
aeronautics 17
Aerospace Research Pilot School 45
Air Transport Auxiliary 33
aircraft 34, 38, 41, 42
airmail 17, 23, 37
airship 4
air show 15, 17
airspeed indicator 20
Alcock, John 5, 18–21
altitude 17, 28, 38, 44
Antoinette IV 16
Atlantic Ocean 18, 20, 22, 24, 28, 36,
Australia 21, 31, 32–33
aviation 5, 26, 38
aviator 5, 14, 22, 26, 30, 42

Bell X-1 43, 44–45
Bell X-1A 44
biplane 11, 13, 35
biplane glider 9
Blériot, Louis 5, 14–17, 23
box kite 7
box-kite plane 12
British Overseas Airways Corporation (BOAC) 41
Brown, Arthur Whitten 5, 18–21

Calais 16
Cayley, George 4, 6–9
co-pilot 24
cockpit 15–16, 20, 44
crash 12, 15–16, 21, 29, 33
crew 19, 28
Curtiss NC-4 19

de Lambert, Charles 15–16

Earhart, Amelia 5, 26–29
engine 5, 8, 11, 15, 17, 20, 23, 31, 35, 38–39, 40–41, 43
engineer 13, 30, 38
engineering 21–22, 34, 38
English Channel 14, 16–17, 24

fighter plane 19, 41
Flyer 11–12, 14
Flyer III 12
flyer 8
flying boat 19, 36
France 7, 14
fuel 19, 23, 29, 33, 40, 44
fuel gauge 20
fuselage 42

generator 20
glider 4, 6–9, 11, 14
Gloster Meteor 41
Gipsy Moth 31

Hargrave, Lawrence 7
Heinkel He 178 39
helicopter 5–6, 34–37
helixpteron 35
Hindenburg 5
Hinkler, Bert 31
hot-air balloon 4, 7
Howland Island 28–29
hydrogen 8

Ireland 20, 24, 28

Jason 31
Jason II 32
jet aircraft 34, 38, 41, 43
jet propulsion 39
Johnson, Amy 5, 30–33

Kitty Hawk 11

Langley, Samuel 11
Latham, Herbert 16–17
Le Grand 35
Leonardo da Vinci 4, 35
Lilienthal, Otto 9, 11
Lillebule 15
Lindbergh, Charles 5, 22–25, 28
Lockheed Electra 28–29
Lockheed Vega 28
London 17, 41
London Aeroplane Club 30

Mach 1 43–44
Messerschmidt Me 262 39–43
Mollison, Jim 32–33
monoplane 14–16, 23
monoplane glider 9
multi-engined plane 34
multiplane 13–14

navigation 9, 21
navigator 19, 29
New York 22–23, 27, 36–37
Newfoundland 19, 24, 28
Ninety-Nines Club 27
Noonan, Fred 29

ornithopter 14
Orteig, Raymond B. 22–23

Pan American Airways 36
Paris 14, 17, 22–23, 34, 37, 41
passenger 17, 28, 34–35, 41
pilot 11, 15, 18, 23, 26–27, 33, 35, 39, 42
propeller 5, 12, 14–15

Royal Air Force (RAF) 19, 21, 33, 41, 43
Cranwell 39, 41
Royal Naval Flying Service (RNFS) 18–19
Ryan NYP 23

Santos-Dumont, Alberto 12
seaplane 18, 40
Sikorsky, Igor 5, 34–37
Smith brothers 21
Sopwith Camel 18
sound barrier 5, 42, 44
speed 17, 32, 41–44
Spirit of St. Louis 23, 25
supersonic 44–45

test pilot 40, 42–44
triplane 13
triplane glider 8

undercarriage 8, 31
United Aircraft Corporation 25, 36
United States Air Force 42–43, 45
USA 10, 23, 25, 29, 33–34, 36, 42

Vickers Vimy 19–21

Whittle, Frank 5, 38–41
wing-warping 11
wings 4, 11, 13–15, 31, 42
World War I 13, 17–19
World War II 25, 39, 42
Wright brothers 4–5, 10–13, 34

Yaeger, Chuck 5, 42–45

HOLY TRINITY SCHOOL LIBRARY
3815 OAK LAWN